A magical art filled alphabet book.

by Ollie and Joon Moon

is for Ant

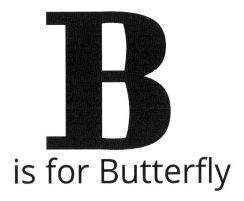

is for Butterfly

C

is for Cat

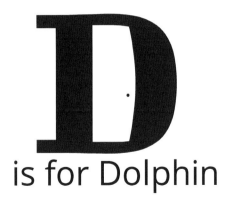

is for Dolphin

is for Elephant

is for Fish

is for Giraffe

is for Hummingbird

is for Iguana

is for Jellyfish

K
is for Kangeroo

is for Lion

is for Mallard

is for Nightingale

is for Octopuss

is for Parrot

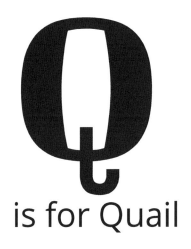

is for Quail

R

is for Racoon

is for Snake

is for Tiger

U

is for Unicorn

is for Vulture

is for Whale

is for Xenosaurus

is for YellowJacket

is for Zebra

Printed in Great Britain
by Amazon

26466782R00032